CONTENTS

SNAKES OF THE FOREST

Eyelash pit vipers come in all
sorts of colours, from yellow
and orange to green and purple.
They are named after the horn-
like scales over each eye.

TROPICAL
RAINFOREST HABITATS
BY
BARBARA TAYLOR

THE LIVING FOREST

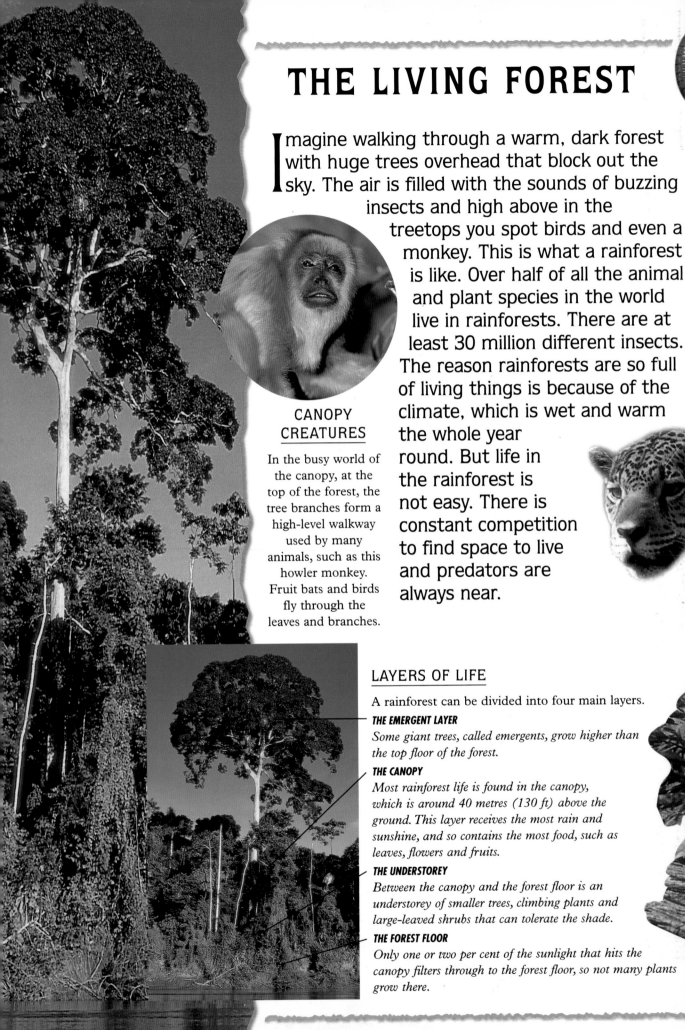

Imagine walking through a warm, dark forest with huge trees overhead that block out the sky. The air is filled with the sounds of buzzing insects and high above in the treetops you spot birds and even a monkey. This is what a rainforest is like. Over half of all the animal and plant species in the world live in rainforests. There are at least 30 million different insects. The reason rainforests are so full of living things is because of the climate, which is wet and warm the whole year round. But life in the rainforest is not easy. There is constant competition to find space to live and predators are always near.

CANOPY CREATURES

In the busy world of the canopy, at the top of the forest, the tree branches form a high-level walkway used by many animals, such as this howler monkey. Fruit bats and birds fly through the leaves and branches.

LAYERS OF LIFE

A rainforest can be divided into four main layers.

THE EMERGENT LAYER
Some giant trees, called emergents, grow higher than the top floor of the forest.

THE CANOPY
Most rainforest life is found in the canopy, which is around 40 metres (130 ft) above the ground. This layer receives the most rain and sunshine, and so contains the most food, such as leaves, flowers and fruits.

THE UNDERSTOREY
Between the canopy and the forest floor is an understorey of smaller trees, climbing plants and large-leaved shrubs that can tolerate the shade.

THE FOREST FLOOR
Only one or two per cent of the sunlight that hits the canopy filters through to the forest floor, so not many plants grow there.

FOREST GIANTS

The year-round warmth of the rainforest means some animals grow into giants, such as the giant millipedes. These look rather alarming but actually feed on dead plant material. Other rainforest giants include the largest frog in the world, the goliath frog, and the largest butterfly, the Queen Alexandra's birdwing butterfly.

FOREST PEOPLES

Kalapolo Indians live in the Brazilian rainforest. People have inhabited rainforests for thousands of years, but little is known about them, or how long they have lived in the forest. Warmth and moisture break down organic materials, such as wood, very quickly, so ancient remains are rare.

LIFE IN THE UNDERSTOREY

Among the tangle of leaves and branches in the understorey live climbing animals. Many are small and light, such as tree frogs, lemurs, coatis and tree snakes like this emerald tree boa. Others are much heavier and have to keep to the larger branches.

THE FOREST FLOOR

Large hunters such as jaguars and tigers prowl along the forest floor. Hogs, peccaries and tapirs dig up bulbs and shoots from the soil, and there are plenty of insects for hungry giant anteaters and tenrecs.

RAINFORESTS OF THE WORLD

WHERE IN THE WORLD?

There are four main areas of rainforest in the world today – in Central and South America, in Africa, in Southeast Asia and in Australasia (shaded dark green on the map, above). Every rainforest in the world is different with many species of plants and animals living only in one area. This is because the continents have drifted apart over millions of years, separating the different areas of rainforest so that the plants and animals developed separately into different forms.

T he word 'rainforest' is used to describe forests that grow in constantly wet conditions. Most rainforests have an annual rainfall of 250 cm (almost 100 inches), that falls evenly throughout the year. Thunderstorms are common in the afternoons. Water given off by the trees adds to the moisture in the air, so the air feels sticky, or humid, and clouds and mist hang over the forest like smoke. This overhead cloud protects the forest from daytime heat and night-time cold, keeping temperatures between 23 °C (73 °F) and 31 °C (88 °F) throughout the year. The hottest, wettest rainforests are located in a narrow belt along the Equator. These are sometimes called lowland rainforests. Rainforests further away from the Equator are just as warm as lowland rainforests, but have a short dry season. Another type of rainforest, called a cloud forest, grows on tropical mountains, while mangrove rainforests grow on some tropical coasts.

COLD AIR

WARM AIR

EQUATOR

RAINFOREST CLIMATE

Rainforests are hot because they grow in a band around the middle of the Earth, called the Equator, where the Sun's rays are at their strongest. The Sun's heat warms the ground, which then warms the air above it. The warm air rises up. As it rises, it cools down and moisture in the air condenses into water droplets, which collect together to make clouds and rain.

MONSOON OR SEASONAL FORESTS

Tropical rainforests with three or more dry months each year are called monsoon forests or seasonal forests. This is because the trees drop their leaves in the dry season and grow new leaves at the start of the wet monsoon season. These forests have fewer climbing plants than lowland rainforests because the air is drier. There are also more plants growing on the forest floor because a lot of light reaches the ground in the dry season.

CLOUD FORESTS

High up on tropical mountains – above 900 metres (3,000 ft) – grow misty forests of twisted, stunted trees covered in bright green mosses and dripping with water. Lichens, ferns, orchids and other plants perch along the branches. These cloud (or montane) forests have fewer plant species than lowland forests, as low temperatures and strong winds make it hard for plants to grow.

MANGROVE FORESTS

Tropical shorelines are often clothed in a special type of rainforest, called a mangrove forest, which does not have a great variety of species. These forests grow on the coasts of the Indian Ocean, the western Pacific Ocean, and also on the shores of the Americas, the Caribbean and West Africa.

WHAT'S THE WEATHER?

Inside a rainforest, the climate, called the micro-climate, varies at different levels, so those animals on the forest floor experience different conditions to those in the canopy. When it rains, the water drips down through the leaves, sometimes taking 10 minutes to reach the ground. When the Sun shines, the air at the top of the canopy is hot and dry, but on the ground it is always warm and damp. A strong wind may be blowing up in the canopy, but at ground level there isn't even a breeze.

THE WATER CYCLE

As rain drips down through the rainforest, the trees and plants take in moisture through their leaves and roots. Unused water evaporates, or disappears through tiny holes in their leaves. Water also evaporates from the ground. All the warm, wet air rises up into the sky, where it cools down to make rain clouds. Rain falls down from the clouds into the forest to start the water cycle all over again.

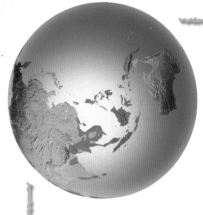

ASIAN FORESTS

Almost 40 per cent of all the rainforest in Asia is to be found in the Indonesian archipelago, and most of the richest mangrove forests occur along South-east Asian coasts.

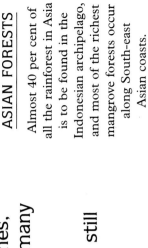

KING COBRA

The largest of all poisonous snakes, king cobras grow to a length of up to 5.5 metres (18 ft). They are actually shy snakes and prefer to keep well away from people. Female king cobras are the only snakes known to build a nest for their eggs.

ASIAN RAINFORESTS

The main area of rainforest in Southeast Asia spreads south from Malaysia to Indonesia. Widespread human destruction of the forests of Southeast Asia has left little of the rainforest in its natural state. Some islands, such as the Philippines, have hardly any rainforest left. Because of this, many of the Asian rainforest species are in danger of extinction, such as the Sumatran rhino and the Vietnam pheasant. Other areas, such as Borneo, still have much of their original forest cover.

MALAYAN TAPIR

The black and white colours of the Malayan tapir help to break up its outline so predators cannot see it in the dark. Tapirs are shy, timid, solitary animals and come out mainly at night. They use their long trunk-like nose to pull tender shoots, buds and fruits from rainforest plants.

ATLAS MOTH

This is one of the largest moths in the world. It has a wingspan of up to 30 cm (12 inches) and is often mistaken for a bird as it flutters around the rainforests of Southeast Asia. Males have huge feathery antennae – the largest of any butterfly or moth – to help them pick up the scent of females among the rainforest trees.

MANGROVE TREES

Mangrove trees grow in salty mud and have a mass of tangled roots to support them in the waterlogged ground. Special breathing roots stick up through the mud into the air to help the roots get enough oxygen. The roots also trap the mud and help to stabilise the coastline and build up new strips of land.

AUSTRALASIAN RAINFORESTS

The largest rainforest in Australasia grows on the island of New Guinea. Most of it is still undisturbed and contains a mixture of Asian and Australasian plants and animals. Australian rainforests are all that remain of a vast rainforest that once covered parts of this continent and Antarctica during much warmer climates millions of years ago. They are not as rich in species as other rainforests but they contain many unique forms of life.

AUSTRALASIAN RAINFORESTS

Australasian rainforests spread up from the northeastern coast of Queensland in Australia to the island of New Guinea.

RAINBOW LORIKEET

Screeching flocks of rainbow lorikeets feed in the upper canopy, lapping up nectar and pollen from flowers with their brush-tipped tongues. They may have to fly long distances in search of flowering trees.

SPOTTED CUSCUS

Eight species of cuscus, including the spotted cuscus, appear in the rainforests of New Guinea. Cuscuses have a partly-bald prehensile tail for gripping branches. At night they feed on leaves, flowers and insects; some species feed in the rainforest canopy, others in the understorey or on the ground.

TREE KANGAROOS

Australasian rainforests do not have monkeys swinging through the trees. Instead, they have tree kangaroos and a variety of marsupials, such as possums and gliders. Tree kangaroos occur mainly on New Guinea, but two species live in Queensland rainforests. Tree kangaroos are different from ground-dwelling kangaroos because they have powerful front legs, short back feet, sharp claws for gripping branches and a long tail. The long tail helps a tree kangaroo to balance on tree branches.

7

AFRICAN RAINFORESTS

THE SAME BUT DIFFERENT

Animals living in rainforests in different parts of the world have sometimes come to look the same because they have adapted to a similar lifestyle. They are different species, but because they live, feed and survive in a similar way, their bodies look similar. This idea is called convergent evolution and some examples are the hornbills of Africa (above) and the toucans of South America (below).

African rainforests contain fewer species than the rain-forests of either America or Asia. This is because many plants and animals died out when the climate of Africa became much drier during the last Ice Age, which ended about 12,000 years ago. Most of the wildlife in Madagascar's rainforests is unique to the island because it has evolved in isolation from Africa for at least 40 million years.

COLOBUS MONKEY

Living in troops of over 50 animals made up of small family groups, black and white colobus monkeys are active during the daytime. They feed on bark, insects, fruit and leaves, leaping from tree to tree. Unlike South American monkeys, African monkeys do not have prehensile, or gripping, tails.

GOLIATH BEETLE

The heaviest of all insects, male goliath beetles weigh from 70-100g (2.5-3.5 oz), which is roughly three times as much as a house mouse. From the tip of the small horns to the end of the abdomen, they are up to 11 cm (4 inches) long. Females are smaller than males.

AFRICAN FORESTS

A belt of tropical rainforest grows across the centre of Africa, from Cameroon and Gabon on the West coast, to Kenya and Tanzania in East Africa. More than 80 per cent of Africa's rainforest is in central Africa. These forests spread out from small patches of forest that survived the dry African climate during the last Ice Age. In East Africa, rainforest grows mainly in mountain regions.

GREY PARROT

Noisy grey parrots whistle and shriek to each other before settling down to roost for the night in groups of 100 or more. They have remarkable powers of mimicry and captive birds can be trained to use human language as a means of communicating intelligently with people.

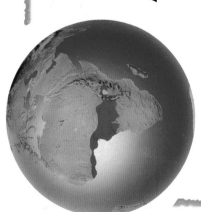

AMERICAN RAINFORESTS

The biggest area of rainforest is in the Amazon basin in South America. It is twice the size of India and ten times the size of France. About 20 per cent of all the world's bird and flowering plant species and ten per cent of all its mammal species live in the Amazon rainforest. Each type of tree may support more than 400 insect species.

AMERICAN RAINFORESTS

The rainforests of the Americas range from the large forests of the Amazon up through Central America and on to some of the islands in the Caribbean. These islands have many unusual species – some found on only one island. Hurricanes, however, often cause damage to the Caribbean rainforests. The relatively tiny rainforests of Central America are rich in species because they grow on a land bridge between two very different continents.

YELLOW ANACONDA

The yellow anaconda is one of the heaviest snakes. It is highly aquatic, hunting fish and caimans in streams and rivers. Anacondas are a type of boa and constrict their prey, squeezing it to death in their strong coils.

BALD UAKARI

With its bare face and head, long shaggy fur and a beard, the bald uakari is a strange-looking monkey indeed. The three species of uakari are the only New World monkeys to have short tails. They rarely leap, because they do not have long tails to help them balance.

MORPHO BUTTERFLY

The shimmery blue colours on the wings of a male morpho butterfly help to attract females and may also serve to dazzle predators when the butterfly needs to escape. The colours are caused by the way the tiny scales on the wings reflect the light.

RAINFOREST PLANTS

Trees provide the physical structure of a rainforest. Their solid trunks support the weight of the canopy and provide climbing frames for creepers. Their roots help to hold the soil together. Rainforest trees are usually 30-50 metres (100-160 ft) tall, with slender trunks, smooth bark and hard wood. Their life span can be from 150 years to 1,400 years. The leaves of rainforest trees, and other rainforest plants, are often thick and leathery with pointed tips called drip tips. The rain runs quickly off these leaves and stops moss from growing and blocking out the light. A rainforest has a huge variety of trees – an area the size of a soccer pitch could hold as many as 200 species.

A SAFE HAVEN

To get nearer to the light, many plants perch high on the branches of the tall trees. Some of these plants, called bromeliads, make a cup-shaped container with their waxy leaves, which can hold many gallons of water. Animals, like this frog, take advantage of these tree-top ponds as safe places for their young.

GROWING SPACE

One of the main problems for rainforest trees is finding a space in which to grow. Strangler figs have solved this problem by taking the place of a tree already standing.

A bird drops a strangler fig seed on a tree branch and the seed sprouts roots and branches.

The strangler's roots reach the ground and it starts to smother the host tree.

The host tree dies away, leaving the fig standing in its place.

STINKBIRDS

The hoatzin of South America smells a lot like cow manure because its stomach is full of fermenting leaves. It is one of the few rainforest birds to feed on leaves, which stay in the hoatzin's stomach for almost two days, making it too heavy to be a good flier.

BUTTRESS ROOTS

The roots of some trees spread out above the ground to form wide, flat wings called buttresses. These buttress roots may extend 5 metres (16 ft) up the trunk. They probably help to support the tall trees, but may also help the tree to feed. They spread widely and send down fine feeding roots into the soil.

CARNIVOROUS PLANTS

Pitcher plants get extra nutrients by catching and digesting insects and other small animals. Some of the pitchers rest on the ground, while others hang like lanterns along the branches of trees. Some even have lids to keep out the rain. Creatures are attracted by the colours and sweet nectar produced around the rim of the pitcher, but fall down the slippery walls into a pool of acidic liquid. The liquid digests the animals' bodies and the plant absorbs the goodness they contain.

PARASITIC PLANTS

Plants need light to make food, but there is not much light on the dark forest floor. Some plants survive here by stealing their food from other plants. The biggest flower in the world, Rafflesia, is a parasitic plant like this. The body of the plant is a network of threads living inside the stems of a vine that hangs down from the trees and trails along the ground. The flower bud pushes its way out through the vine's bark and then expands to form a flower up to 1 metre (3 ft) across.

PLANT PARTNERS

AVOCADO BIRD

The quetzal feeds on at least 18 different species of avocado, and the avocado trees and the birds need each other to survive. The quetzals swallow the avocado fruit whole but the hard seed passes through the bird's gut unharmed. A new tree can grow from the seed, so the quetzal spreads avocado trees through the forest. If the avocado trees are cut down, or stop fruiting, the quetzals usually disappear from the area.

Most flowering plants need pollen to produce seeds. This pollen has to come from another plant of the same kind. But in the rainforest there is very little wind, so the plants rely on animals to transport the pollen. Animals such as birds, bats and monkeys are useful for spreading pollen because they constantly move over large areas of the forest. Flowers and seeds often sprout directly from trunks or branches to make contact more easily with bats and other large animals, without all the leaves getting in the way. Bat flowers are large, pale and smelly, so bats can find them in the dark, while bird flowers are brilliant colours because birds have good colour vision. Some insects, especially ants, have more complex relationships with rainforest plants – they live right inside the plants and help them to survive.

PERFUME FOR POLLEN

The bucket orchid of Central America goes to amazing lengths to make sure iridescent male bees carry its pollen from flower to flower. To lure the bees into its watery trap, the bucket orchid produces a perfume that the male bees use to attract female bees during courtship. While scraping perfume off the orchid's petals, the bees sometimes slip and fall down into the bucket.

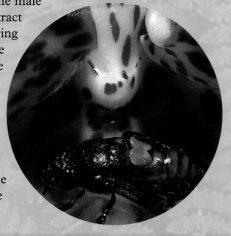

As they escape, they either pick up a new load of pollen or deposit pollen they are already carrying. The pollen is the two lumps stuck to the bee's back like a yellow rucksack (right).

SPREADING SEEDS

Living inside the stems and branches of some rainforest plants are colonies of ants. The plants provide the ants with a home and the ants provide the plants with much needed nutrients in their droppings and the remains of their insect meals. Ant plants are often perched high on tree branches, so they cannot get nutrients from the soil to help them grow. The ants may also defend the plants by biting and stinging animals that try to eat them. This ant plant has holes in the surface of its swollen, prickly stem through which its ant lodgers scurry in and out of their living home. As the ants move about the forest, they help to spread the seeds of the ant plant.

GREEN FUR

The greenish colour of the sloth's fur is provided by tiny plants called algae which lives in the damp hair. Sloths never clean their fur so the algae do not get washed off, and they benefit by living high in the trees, near to the light. With green fur, sloths blend into the leafy green background of the forest so the algae camouflages them from predators. The algae also helps another creature. A tiny moth lays its eggs in the sloth's green fur and its caterpillars feed on the algae.

BEETLE MESSENGERS

To attract beetles for pollination, the *Philodendron* plant produces a strong scent which travels great distances. The flowers even heat up to help the scent evaporate and disperse into the air. The beetles feed and mate inside the flower, then fly off covered with pollen to another *Philodendron* flower.

MOVING THROUGH THE TREES

FLYING LIZARD

In the Southeast Asian rainforests, lizards are some of the most common gliders. Their gliding flaps are made of a thin layer of skin joined to their ribs. These lizards can glide for up to 15 metres (50 ft) between trees, and even change position and roll over while in the air. Gliders make easy targets for hungry birds so many are camouflaged or come out at night when it is harder for predators to see them on the move.

Even with special climbing equipment, it is difficult for people to reach the top of rainforest trees. However, rainforest animals spend their lives swinging, climbing and gliding through the trees. These animals have adapted long arms for swinging, tails for gripping and hanging and sticky toes or long claws for extra grip. Short, rounded wings help birds to twist and turn in the air, while hummingbirds can hover in front of flowers on their small, pointed wings. Some animals glide from tree to tree instead of leaping. Webs or flaps of skin increase the surface area of the body and slow down the glider's fall, like a living parachute. There is even a flying snake which can glide for distances of more than 50 metres (165 ft).

CLINGING CLAWS

The strong claws of a sloth work like hooks to allow the animal to spend much of its time hanging upside down from the branches of trees – even when it is asleep or dead. The claws make a hook over the tree branches. The sloth's slow lifestyle requires very little effort unlike the speedy swinging of the monkeys and apes.

GRIPPING TAILS

Many rainforest animals, from tree porcupines and tree anteaters to kinkajous and woolly monkeys, have a special sort of tail for curling around branches like a hook. This is called a prehensile tail and it is most commonly found in South American monkeys. For some unknown reason, the monkeys of Africa and Southeast Asia have not developed with this useful adaptation. Most monkeys with prehensile tails use them as a third arm, for holding and gathering their food, as well as for moving.

HAIRY SWINGER

With their long arms and strong fingers and toes, orang-utans move easily through the trees, using their feet as well as their hands for climbing. To travel fast, they swing hand over hand in a technique called 'brachiating'. Older male orang-utans are too heavy to do this, but females and young have no trouble with this high speed travel. A female orang-utan has an armspan of about 2.4 metres (almost 8 ft) and can cover large distances quickly.

GLUED TO THE SPOT

Tree frogs, such as this red-eyed tree frog, have special pads under the toes that produce a sticky substance called mucus. Their sticky toes help them to grip wet leaves and other slippery and slimy surfaces as they climb through the trees.

JAGUAR

COLLARED PECCARY

GRASS, ROOTS,
BULBS & WORMS

One of the links between rainforest plants and animals is through their feeding habits. All food chains start with plants because they make their own food, and then the plant-eaters (herbivores), in turn are eaten by meat-eaters, (carnivores).

HIDDEN KILLER

Curled up among the leaves of the forest floor, the gaboon viper is well camouflaged as it waits for a tasty small animal to wander past. Then it leaps out and grabs hold of its prey in a surprise attack. Gaboon vipers kill their prey by biting it with their poisonous fangs. They have the longest fangs of any snake – each one is up to 5 cm (2 inches) long. A snake's teeth are good for holding prey, but not for chopping or chewing, so snakes swallow their prey whole.

PREDATORS & PREY

Rainforest predators are usually small animals because there are not enough large plant-eaters in the forest for large meat-eaters to eat. The exceptions to this are the large cats, such as the jaguar and the tiger, which hunt pigs, antelope and deer on the forest floor. Ground-dwelling snakes also lie in wait for their prey on the forest floor, while tree-dwelling snakes lurk among the branches. Other ground predators include troops of bush dogs in South America and sloth bears in southern India and Sri Lanka. Sky hunters include the fierce hawks and eagles that swoop down into the canopy to seize monkeys and sloths in their strong talons.

TERRIBLE TEETH

Some piranha fish, such as red-bellied piranhas, are lethal killers, biting off slices of flesh from their victims with razor-sharp teeth. They have powerful jaws. Meat-eating piranhas have been known to attack animals as large as goats, which have fallen into the water. But all piranhas live on fruit and nuts for most of the year and some are completely vegetarian.

FELINE HUNTER

Small, agile forest cats, such as this South American margay, are skilled climbers that prey on small rodents, birds and lizards in the trees. Most of them are nocturnal hunters and their yellow or brownish fur with spotted or striped markings gives them good camouflage. Keen sight, hearing and smell enable them to track down their victims, which they kill with a bite to the neck.

SNAPPING JAWS

The caimans of Central and South America have sharper, longer teeth than alligators. They lurk in the water, waiting to snap up fish, frogs or thirsty animals that come down to the forest rivers for a drink. Caimans have strong, bony plates in their back and belly scales for protection against their own predators.

TONGUE ZAPPER

Insects are a major source of food for many rainforest predators, from birds and bats, to tarantula spiders and chameleons. Chameleons flick out their incredibly long tongues at lightning speed to trap insects, spiders, scorpions and other prey on the sticky tip. To search for food, a chameleon can swivel its eyes in all directions. Their movements can be so slow that they are hardly noticeable, especially since the chameleon can change colour to blend with its surroundings.

FOOD CHAIN

BENTWING BAT

⬇

INSECTS

⬇

FLOWERS

This food chain from an Australian rainforest has three links. Should any link be destroyed it will affect the rest of the chain, and all the other food chains in the large and complex food web.

DEFENCE

Rainforest animals use all kinds of different defences to stop themselves being eaten. Sometimes it is possible to run, leap, fly or glide away from a predator, but hiding or blending in with the background is often more successful. Many rainforest insects look just like leaves, twigs or bark, and as long as they keep still they are hard to detect. Certain spiders even disguise themselves as bird droppings. Poisonous animals often have bright warning colours to tell predators to keep away. Some non-poisonous butterflies, such as postman butterflies, copy the colours of poisonous species to trick predators. Another way animals may defend themselves is by putting up a fight.

ANGRY PIGS

The giant forest hog is the largest wild pig and is feared by forest peoples for its bad temper. It has well developed lower canine teeth that stick out of the sides of the mouth to form tusks. Males have larger tusks than females.

SPIDER SURVIVAL

This tarantula makes itself look as frightening as possible to scare predators away. Spiders use their poisonous fangs for defence and tarantulas also flick irritating hairs at attackers. A few spiders look just like stinging insects such as wasps or ants so predators are tricked into leaving them alone. Spiders will even pretend to be dead, since predators prefer to eat living prey.

HIDE AND SEEK

Insects are a major source of food in the rainforest so they have developed many unusual colours, patterns and shapes to pretend they are not nice, tasty snacks. Dead leaves are a good disguise to adopt and leaf insects often have veins and tattered edges just like the real thing.

FROG POISONS

Poison dart frogs have deadly poisons in their skin and are brightly coloured to warn potential predators to keep away. They make some of these poisons themselves but also obtain some from their food, such as toxic insects. Their poisons are so powerful that a tiny smear from its skin is enough to kill a horse. A few Amazonian tribes use this poison on the tips of their blowpipe darts for hunting.

NESTS, EGGS & YOUNG

Rainforests are full of food and places to live, but animals still have to compete for safe nesting sites and protect their young from predators. The warm temperatures help the young to develop and survive the early, vulnerable stages of their lives but the constant rain can make life miserable. Birds protect their eggs and young inside nests or tree holes, while marsupial mothers, such as tree kangaroos or possums, carry their young around with them for months in furry pouches. Even tarantulas guard their eggs until they hatch. But mammals, such as monkeys, cats and bats, take the greatest care of their young, teaching them how to feed, hunt and survive in the forest.

STRIPES & SPOTS

Brazilian tapirs are a plain brown colour but their young have spots and stripes on their fur. This helps to camouflage them so they blend into the background as they move through the rainforest. The markings also break up the outline of the young animal's body so it is harder to see.

CLINGING BABIES

A female orang-utan usually gives birth to a single baby every three to six years. The baby rides on its mother's back as she swings through the trees and sleeps in the same nest at night. Baby orang-utans are totally dependent on their mothers for the first 18 months of their lives. Mother orang-utans do not mate again until their young are at least three years old so a female may only have two or three babies during her lifetime.

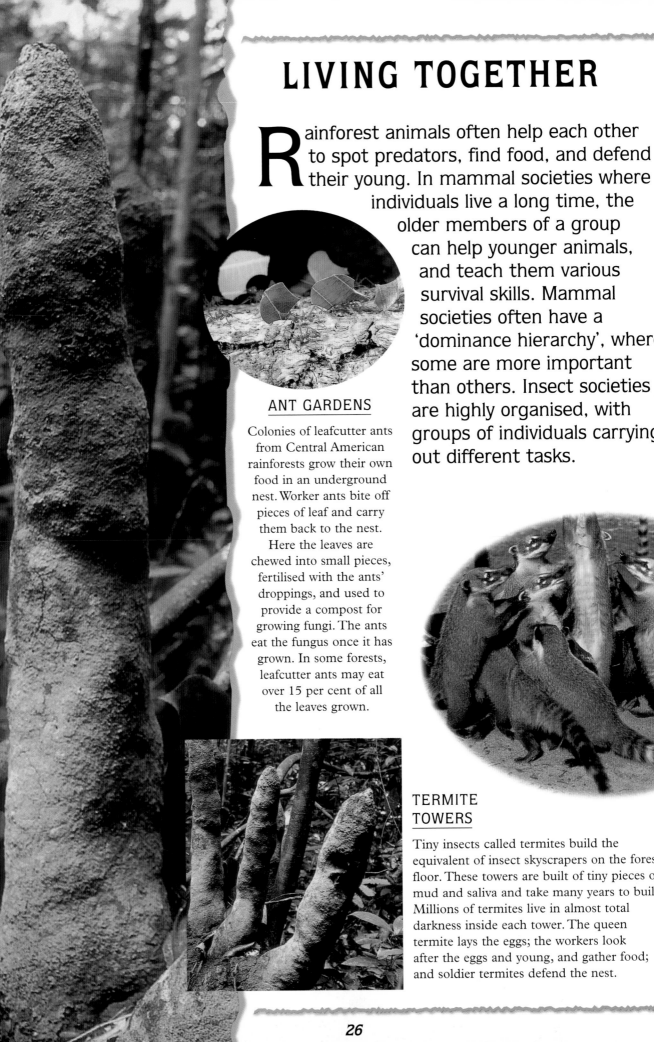

LIVING TOGETHER

Rainforest animals often help each other to spot predators, find food, and defend their young. In mammal societies where individuals live a long time, the older members of a group can help younger animals, and teach them various survival skills. Mammal societies often have a 'dominance hierarchy', where some are more important than others. Insect societies are highly organised, with groups of individuals carrying out different tasks.

ANT GARDENS

Colonies of leafcutter ants from Central American rainforests grow their own food in an underground nest. Worker ants bite off pieces of leaf and carry them back to the nest. Here the leaves are chewed into small pieces, fertilised with the ants' droppings, and used to provide a compost for growing fungi. The ants eat the fungus once it has grown. In some forests, leafcutter ants may eat over 15 per cent of all the leaves grown.

TERMITE TOWERS

Tiny insects called termites build the equivalent of insect skyscrapers on the forest floor. These towers are built of tiny pieces of mud and saliva and take many years to build. Millions of termites live in almost total darkness inside each tower. The queen termite lays the eggs; the workers look after the eggs and young, and gather food; and soldier termites defend the nest.

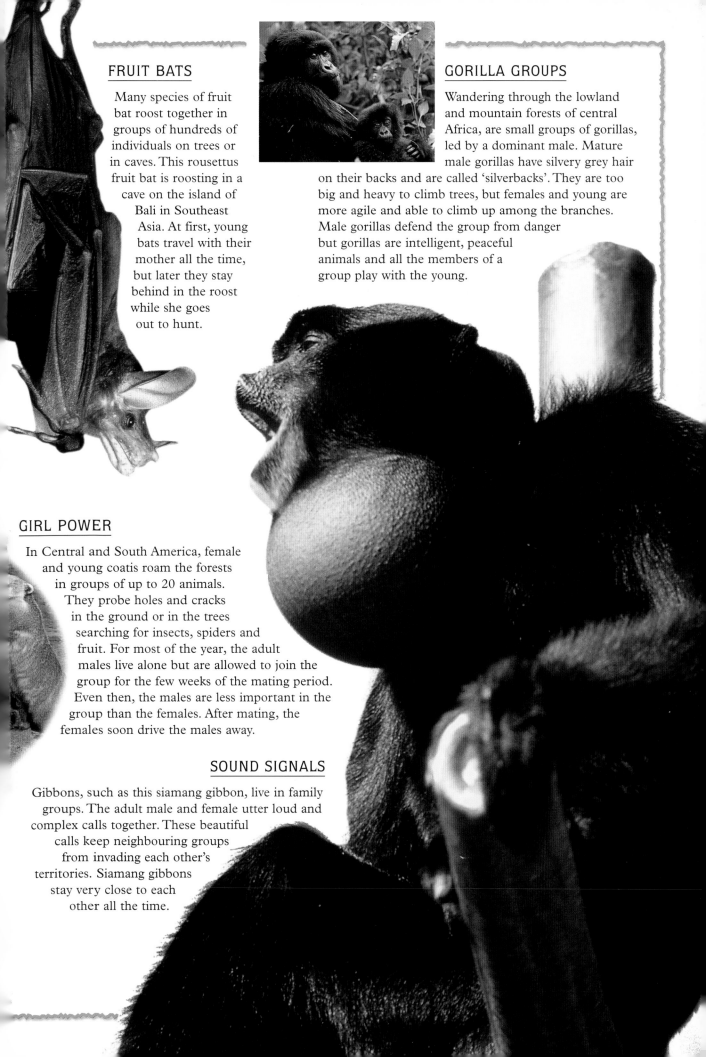

FRUIT BATS

Many species of fruit bat roost together in groups of hundreds of individuals on trees or in caves. This rousettus fruit bat is roosting in a cave on the island of Bali in Southeast Asia. At first, young bats travel with their mother all the time, but later they stay behind in the roost while she goes out to hunt.

GORILLA GROUPS

Wandering through the lowland and mountain forests of central Africa, are small groups of gorillas, led by a dominant male. Mature male gorillas have silvery grey hair on their backs and are called 'silverbacks'. They are too big and heavy to climb trees, but females and young are more agile and able to climb up among the branches. Male gorillas defend the group from danger but gorillas are intelligent, peaceful animals and all the members of a group play with the young.

GIRL POWER

In Central and South America, female and young coatis roam the forests in groups of up to 20 animals. They probe holes and cracks in the ground or in the trees searching for insects, spiders and fruit. For most of the year, the adult males live alone but are allowed to join the group for the few weeks of the mating period. Even then, the males are less important in the group than the females. After mating, the females soon drive the males away.

SOUND SIGNALS

Gibbons, such as this siamang gibbon, live in family groups. The adult male and female utter loud and complex calls together. These beautiful calls keep neighbouring groups from invading each other's territories. Siamang gibbons stay very close to each other all the time.

PEOPLES OF THE RAINFOREST

For thousands of years, the world's rainforests have been home to groups of people who have a deep understanding of the forests. Their knowledge of the rainforest's plants and animals, and their ability to use a wide range of foods and natural medicines, are the key to their survival but population densities have never been high. Some rainforest peoples live in small patches of forest for a while before moving on. Unfortunately, as forests are cleared for their timber or their land, the homes of forest peoples are destroyed, or they are killed by diseases, such as measles, introduced by settlers from outside the forest.

NEW GUINEA PEOPLES

The New Guinea highlanders decorate themselves in magnificent costumes for special occasions and perform complicated dances. They paint their faces and bodies in vivid colours. The pattern often has something to do with religious beliefs and ancestral spirits.

HUNTING WEAPONS

This Mentawai man from Indonesia is carrying his bow and arrow along with some stripped bark. To capture monkeys, birds and other prey high in the canopy, rainforest hunter-gatherers use poisoned arrows or darts. The poisons he uses come from plant juices or the skin of poisonous tree frogs, and sometimes hunters have to wait for hours before the animal dies and falls out of the trees.

PYGMIES

The Pygmies of Africa have adapted physically to their way of life as hunter-gatherers in the forest. Their small size makes it easier to move about in the undergrowth and they have a light muscular build which is well suited to tree climbing. Some tribes of pygmies seem to be completely at home in the tree tops, often climbing to reach the nests of wild bees to collect the honey. A small bird called a honeyguide often leads the hunters to a hive. The hunter helps the bird by opening the hive and leaves it a meal of beeswax as a reward.

NUMBERS OF PEOPLE

A large area of rainforest can support only a few hundred people. If the Mbuti pygmies spread themselves evenly across their rainforest in Africa, there would be one for every 4 sq km (1.5 sq miles). So rainforest peoples are spread thinly through the forest. Some build houses to settle for a time and many families may live in the same house.

FOREST TRANSPORT

In dense forest, it is easier to travel along rivers than to move through the undergrowth. Dugout canoes are often used for transport, but making them takes a long time. A tree has to be felled and then cut and hollowed out with an axe. Pieces of wood called stretchers are placed across the canoe to prevent it warping. When the canoe is finished, a fire is lit underneath and inside the canoe to harden and seal the wood.

SHIFTING CULTIVATION

Also called 'slash-and-burn', shifting cultivation is well suited to the poor soils of a rainforest. The people cut down and burn a small area of forest so the nutrients in the plants enrich the soil for a while and weeds are destroyed. Then they plant seeds, and as the crops grow, the plot needs constant weeding, since weeds grow well in the warm, wet conditions. Eventually, the weeds overcome the crops and the goodness in the soil is used up so the people move on to another patch of forest. Cultivated areas are left to lie fallow (rest and recover), for between 8 and 20 years. Shifting cultivation does not cause any lasting harm to the forest.

CEREMONIES

Many rainforest peoples paint their bodies with colourful dyes and use feathers, flowers and other natural materials to make jewellery. Men, such as this Cofan Indian from Ecuador, are sometimes the only ones allowed to wear full ceremonial costume. There are strong traditions of dance and ceremony and special occasions such as weddings, funerals and harvests are marked by dances and feasts.

PROTECTING THE RAINFOREST

Rainforests have taken millions of years to become the complex environments that they are today. They are very fragile because every part depends on every other part. Unfortunately, most rainforests are in poor countries, which need to make money from resources like timber. But clearing the rainforests causes many problems such as soil erosion, floods, droughts, extinction of species and the disturbance of forest peoples. About half of all the rainforests in the world have already been cut down and an area about the size of a football pitch disappears every second. Much more could be done to save the world's rainforests. Timber companies could replace the trees they cut down, or grow plantations of valuable rainforest trees. More large areas of rainforest could also be preserved as national parks.

TIMBER!

With chain saws, diggers and powerful machinery, logging companies can clear huge areas of rainforest in a frighteningly short time. It takes several hundred years for a rainforest tree to grow taller than an electricity pylon and only a few minutes for a man to chop it down with a chainsaw. Roads have to be built to get the machinery into the forest and, as the valuable timber trees are scattered throughout the forest, great holes have to be torn in the forest to reach each one. Loggers usually destroy three times as many trees as they harvest.

OUT INTO THE WILD

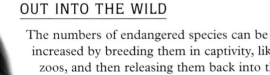

The numbers of endangered species can be increased by breeding them in captivity, like zoos, and then releasing them back into the wild. This is not a simple process as the animals have never been in a natural rainforest and have to learn how to survive. Scientists have fitted these tamarins with radio collars so they can follow their movements through the forest. In 1908, only about 100 golden lion tamarins survived in the wild, but conservation work has now increased numbers to about 400.

MEDICINAL PLANTS

These Antanosy girls are holding a rosy periwinkle plant, which is used for making drugs to treat certain types of cancer. The plant grows in the rapidly disappearing rainforests of Madagascar and may soon become an endangered species. Many other rainforest plants could contain useful drugs but they may become extinct before they are discovered. Twenty per cent of all drugs contain extracts of rainforest plants, yet only one per cent of rainforest plants have been tested.

RAINFOREST RESEARCH

Although rainforest people have vast knowledge about plants and animals in the forest, scientists also need to collect information for conservation projects. Millions of species need to be identified and the complex web of life better understood to work out how best to preserve the rainforests for the future. Since it is difficult to travel through the forest, some researchers float over the forest in airships to take samples from the canopy.

PROTECTED SPECIES

Large sums of money can be made from selling endangered animals and plants. International laws are meant to protect rare species but it is often difficult to enforce these laws. The jaguar is fully protected under the CITES (Convention on International Trade in Endangered Species) but people still want its skin. Often the people who catch the animals make very little money from the trade, with the traders making most of the profit. If people refuse to buy goods made from protected species, this will help stop the animals being killed.

GLOSSARY

Archipelago A group or chain of islands, usually found in open ocean.

Australasia The region made up of the countries of New Zealand, Australia and islands of the South West Pacific Ocean.

Brachiating A method of swinging from tree to tree using one hand over the other.

Courtship A ritual whereby an adult of a species selects another to mate with.

Equator An imaginary line that runs around the middle of the planet, dividing the Earth into northern and southern hemispheres.

Gliders Small mammals that have a special wing-like flap of skin connected to their wrists and ankles, enabling them to glide from tree to tree.

Marsupials Mammals with pouches on their front, which baby marsupials live in when they are first born.

Pollination The part of a flower's life cycle when pollen is transferred to it, allowing it to develop seeds and reproduce.

Prehensile tail The tail of an animal which has adapted to be able to grasp and hold objects.

Regurgitate The process performed by some birds where they bring up food they have swallowed to feed their young, or mate.

ACKNOWLEDGMENTS

We would like to thank: Ben Hubbard. Artwork by Peter Bull Art Studio.

Copyright © 2009 *ticktock* Entertainment Ltd

First published in Great Britain by *ticktock* Media Ltd, The Old Sawmill, 103 Goods Station Road,

Tunbridge Wells, Kent TN1 2DP, Great Britain

All rights reserved. No part of this publication may be reproduced, stored in a retrieval system, or transmitted in any form or by any means electronic, mechanical, photocopying, recording or otherwise, without prior written permission of the copyright owner.

A CIP catalogue record for this book is available from the British Library.

ISBN 978 1 84898 006 8 (paperback)

ISBN 978 1 84898 051 8 (hardback)

Picture research by Image Select. Printed in China.

Picture Credits: t=top, b=bottom, c=centre, l=left, r=right, OFC=outside front cover, OBC=outside back cover, IFC=inside front cover

B&C Alexander; 28/29c, 29cr. Bruce Coleman Limited; 12/13b, 14tr, 20tl. Colorific; 3c. Jacana; 2tl, 6bl, 7tr, 7br, 8cr, 10/11t, 11tr, 12tl, 13r, 14bl, 17tr, 18c, 18/19c, 19b, 21br, 26/27c, 27b, 31br, OBCbl. Oxford Scientific Films; IFC, 12br, 19tc, 22tl, 24br, 26tl. Planet Earth Pictures; 2l & 2bl, 3/4b, 3tr, 3/4t, 4/5c, 4/5b, 5br, 6br, 6c, 6tr, 7bl, 8tl, 8tr, 8c, 8br, 9t, 9c, 9cr, 10l, 10tl, 11c, 11b, 14/15b, 15br, 16tl, 16bl, 17c & 32, 17b, 18tl, 18bl, 19tr, 20bl, 20cr, 21tl, 21c, 21tr, 22c, 22cl, 22/23ct, 23tr, 23cl, 23br, 24/25c, 24bl, 25tr, 25br, 26l & 26bl, 26/27t, 27t, 28tl, 28bl, 29br, 30tl, 30bl, 30/31c, 31tr, OBCbr. P.I.X; 15t. Shutterstock; OFC. Tony Stone; 29cl.

Every effort has been made to trace the copyright holders and we apologise in advance for any unintentional omissions. We would be pleased to insert the appropriate acknowledgement in any subsequent edition of this publication.

INDEX